Spoken From A Rambling Mind

Thoughts, Poems, and Nonsense

Carol MT Slavens

BookLeaf Publishing

India | USA | UK

Made with ❤ on the BookLeaf Publishing Platform
www.bookleafpub.in
www.bookleafpub.com

Dedication

To all those that have touched my life, no matter how long or short they remained; and also for all of the souls who have taken a part in the shape of mine.

.

.

Preface

My mind can be crazy! But I have so many thoughts that seem so depthless. I can't always verbalize, but I'm happy to share some of my plague. The plague of a rambling mind. Enjoy!

Acknowledgements

Too many to count!

1. No One Dies Alone

I will walk with you to death's door.
I will hold your hand while you cross into that void.
I cannot come with you, as this is the final journey.
Everyone who knocks this door must cross the threshold
alone.

I will sit with you.
Cry with you.
I will hold your hand.
Support your soul.
Until you are greeted by Death's embrace.

If you are met by one's gone ahead,
Even if embraced by only death himself.

I may not know you long.
I may only know a part of your story.
But no one should die alone.

2. Demons

Confront your demons.
Square up.
Fight them.
Keep them in your mind's eye.
Shove them off that cliff.

You can run. . .
but the unfortunate thing,
Things that haunt you?
they will always follow.
They will always catch up.
Eventually.

You're stronger than you know.
You are more powerful than you realize.
You've become equipped for this.
You've worked too hard to flee.

Breathe in those demons,
Breathe out that release.

Freedom.
Fight.

Believe in your skill.
Have faith in your strength.
You've fought this least once before.
Do it again.

3. ADHD

Mind is chaotic
Zoning out is cathartic.

When the mind has traffic
Sit back in a hammock

Relaxing ain't happening
Anxieties continuously spring

Best to ignore them
Maybe I just need some stim'

Panic isn't right
Supplement with a quiet night

Maybe distraction
Can break the traction

ADHD
You sick son-of-a-B

4. More Than Affirmations

I hope you know that one day you will be okay again.
I hope you come to realize that one moment not seized
won't greatly impact your overall good.
I hope you know that you've made a difference in
someone's life.
I hope you know that the imprint you leave behind is
cherished.
I hope you know that you are strong and you are
capable.
I hope you know that your soul has wings that can carry
you tp any wind you choose.
I hope you know that it is alright to change your mind,
and then change it again.
I hope you know that you can give yourself grace.
I hope you know that it is perfectly normal to fall apart
sometimes.
I hope you know that your strength is unmatched.
I hope, most of all, that you know that you are
important:

5. Miss you

Maybe the clouds will turn a little more white
Maybe my soul will remember how to feel
Maybe my chest will feel a bit less tight
Maybe these feelings will find a place to spill

I know the sky is still blue
and the sun keeps its golden hue
But I'm stuck in this winter dead.
Because the sun left when you did.

I have only one question to inquire.
Are you happy out there?
Did you find all that fed your fire?
Are you chasing those storms somewhere?

Okay, I have more questions than one.
So much more left unsaid.
Needless to say,
I'll miss you until the sun is dead.

6. Differences

I hope we don't stop noticing everyone's differences.
I hope we don't tell people "we're all humans, we're all the same".
We. Are. Not.
What needs to change is grouping and separating people because of their differences.
We should have no shame in noticing that someone has a different physical trait.
The shame comes when we stereotype and place everyone with a similar trait in a group.
Differences should be noticed.
Differences should be celebrated.
Just like experiences.
Imagine if people were grouped only by their experiences... no progress would ever be made. So.
Notice those differences.
Celebrate differences.
Ask questions about those differences.
Take no offense when people ask you about that trait that makes you stand apart.

Have no fear in educating yourself on those differences.
Celebrate the breaks in the mundane and "average"
because within those cracks lie the facets of beauty that
we are suppressing and suffocating.
We are all uniquely impressive.
That should not be smudged out.

7. Love's Companion

Love does not roam free.
No, in fact, it carries quite a charge.

Love comes with a bitter companion.
Grief.
Grief, loss, is the closest companion to love.

While love is beautiful and sought by all,
It is not without cost.

Like the darkness wouldn't be without the light,
Love wouldn't be without the grief.

For a heart that is hurting,
Is a heart that's been deeply loved.

8. Grit

Grit isn't about wit
Or about the words that you spit.

Grit sets you apart
Keeps your feet at the start.

Grit gives you the resistance
To hold strong in your existence.

Grit may come across as abrasive,
But it keeps out the persuasive.

Grit gives the soul feet,
To stand in the world and not cheat.

Grit holds tight to convictions,
And takes aim against addictions.

Grit is made by experience,
Yes, this makes all the difference.

Grit sets one apart,
Encourages heart.

There is no shame in being gritty,
Ask for no pity.

You've got grit;
Don't you dare lose it.

9. Life

Living is like a roiling sky,
Equal parts dark and light.
Sometimes clear and care free,
Other times wild and disordered.
Perhaps this explains those 'winds of change'.

The same way every day must end,
So must every storm.
A tempest can be cleansing.
A sun-filled day can scald.
Clouds may bring hazardous squalls,
Winds may clear the air.

Embrace the chaos that is living.
Be restless in your search for passion.
Love fiercely but fight furiously.
Above all, learn as much as you can.
LIVE your beautiful, tumultuous, unpredictable
LIFE.

10. Heart of Healthcare

The heart of healthcare service is hardened,
Jaded.
It has been broken more times than anyone can
Tally.
It has bled internally and outwardly showcased
Strength.
It has wept for the patients, and for those they leave
Behind.
It has watched while corporate heads prioritized
Profit.
It has been left speechless and helpless
Often.
It has trudged on through the trenches of the
Unknown.
It came into this world with thoughts of only upmost
Care.
It was designed as a placed to help one
Heal.
It has undergone criticism from those who do not
Know.

It is armored against all of these things with internal
Walls.
Underneath it all, though, the heart of healthcare is
Soft.
Battered and bruised, this heart will go on;
Forever.
The heart of healthcare may be wounded, but it will
Persevere.

11. Wanderer

Death, the lonely wanderer
Forever roaming the realms in search of
Souls to bring home
They're never to stay with him,
They're likely to run
Most live in fear of the day he knocks
But death is no one to fear
He is a friend who guides all to the end.
For the souls who take his hand,
There will be no suffering.
The pain and grief is left to those who stay behind.
And so he remains a lonely force.
Always around, mostly unpredictable,
But hovering close all the same

12. Light

You are a bright spot in this world
Yours is a pocket of light for only some to see
You cannot know all
You will not know all
But you will leave a touch on those you meet.
Your light is the softened edge of
The hard life you've lived.
Your journey is for you to keep
Your lessons for you to decipher
But your light
Your light is yours to share.
In your moments of doubt just know
You ARE a bright space in this
Otherwise dark and empty place.

13. Short

Life's too short
It's too early to abort.
So let's not get too sappy
And just try to live happy.
Oh, for just awhile
Can we sit in denial?
Yes, the world whips around fast
But why dwell on the past?
Can't we find a way to forgive
Instead of our traumas relive ?
Just for a moment
Can we let joy be more potent?
Let us dance in the rain,
Be just a little insane
For life only comes once
Don't you waste it, you dunce.
Life is too short, too short, too short.

14. Don't end up alone

Sometimes things just work out
Other times they simply don't
This doesn't mean you'll forever live without
It just means you got more to hone
it takes meticulous care for things to sprout
But it takes almost nothing to reduce it to bone
Don't spend your worries on doubt
Don't let that heart turn to stone
It isn't a crime to be stout
Take care, and you won't end up alone

15. Fierce

Never fear your aptitude to be fierce
Sometimes necessary is a soul that can pierce
It is not indicative of an inability to feel
No, for the fierce emotions are hard to bring to heel
It is all about the passion
So much that the world will never be ashen
It is not about being brave
It is is not about taking brute strength to the grave
Ferocity is built
It is not without guilt
But it is grounded in love
Something impossible to shove
Always the empath
Use this strength to hit the world with a splash

16. Write

Oh what if we could write
Stay so contrite
About the past we've lived
About the time that ran fast
And left us behind
We came out ahead, forward,
But it's easy to feel left so far in tow
It is okay to mourn ourselves
The children we were
And the adults we became
Tomorrow will bring change
And still we will have pride and love
For yesterdays soul

17. What a Day

Wow what a day
It came in such a way
Is she to blame; the moon ?
Or are we just judging too soon
It comes in threes
Such are the decrees
I've never known what to say
About such a day
Goodness isn't far
So why does it seem like we're walking through tar
All we see is the bad
Looking for any reason to be sad
But that's the way of the world
We are all tossed and twirled
So enjoy the ride
Hold joy in grips that can't be pried

18. The Usher

We usher you in to life
And we accompany you out of it.
We miss a lot of the in-between
But get glimpses here and there.
We laugh with you.
We cry with you.
We are pained by your suffering
And we are thrilled by your overcomings.
We are support for your family
And a foundation for you.
We are at times a great punching bag
Or a person who is just there.
We will bring you laughs.
We will bring you tears .
The same you will bring to us.
Regardless of all of this
We will be there for you on your worst day;
And again for your best.
We don't need your thanks
Yes it is appreciated all the same.

What we do is beyond challenging at times
But we all have our reasons to stay.
We are nurses
And we are with you until the end.

19. If The Stars Could Speak

What if the stars could speak?
Imagine the stories they could tell
Imagine the knowledge they could bestow
Millions and billions of years
Watching creation
Watching destruction
Seeing growth
Seeing decay
Imagine the answers they would hold
These beautiful lights that for us never change
They could be watchers
Yes, what if the stars could speak?
What if we would we listen?

20. So What if it Doesn't

So many plans made
So many things to work out

So what if they don't?

So many friends to make
So many lovers to find
So much has to happen

So what if it doesn't?

So many careers to be had
So many goals to bring to fruition
So many, many things to accomplish in this life

So what if you don't?

Life is full of fluidity
You'll never be ready
Change after change will rock that boat you spent all of

your dreams on

So what if it does?

The answers to all of the 'why' questions cannot be
answered in one life.
Happiness and fullness are what we all seek at the end of
the day.
So what if you don't become an astronaut veterinarian
like you dreamed as a kid?

So what if you do?

Embrace the white waters of life.
Be submerged.
Drown a little.
You'll never be able to prepare anyways.
But you know what?

So what if you were happy despite of it all?

21. Until The Brutal End

There is almost always a brutal truth to the reality in which we live. There is foreshadowing of events to come... but with only an unclear picture.

We can guess endlessly why we received the cards we were dealt, but these guesses bring nothing but bitterness. A dull longing accompanied by doubt himself. Sour. Bitter.

... "Until the bitter end", a phrase so often spoken. Yet we don't get to know if the bitterness spoken of is for those who've ended ... or for those they've left behind.

Who can know what lies beyond the bright light and dark curtain close that we all ultimately succumb to?

I personally dream of satin pillows and a velvet landing. I dream of an open countryside in the summer. I dream to meet again the ones who departed before I was ready. A piece of me taken every time. I selfishly try to believe in something that I've grown to doubt.. Something I was taught my entire time in this reality. Doubt is inevitable.

But still I dream of fallen roses and pipers playing. A massive hug and laughter so intense my insides ache. I dream of a happy place where warm thoughts are all that's welcome. All else is banished.

Yet...
There is almost always a brutal truth to end the reality in which we live.